P9-EMK-604

Military Aircraft Library
Navy Strike Planes

Military Aircraft Library
Navy Strike Planes

DR. DAVID BAKER

Rourke Enterprises, Inc.
Vero Beach, FL 32964

Library of Congress Cataloging-in-Publication Data

Baker, David, 1944-
Navy strike planes/by David Baker.

p. cm. — (The Military aircraft series)
Includes index.
Summary: Describes the development and special features of the Navy strike plane, flown exclusively from aircraft carriers, and its uses in battle.
ISBN 0-86592-534-8
1. Fighter planes — United States — Juvenile literature
2. Attack planes — United States — Juvenile literature.
3. United States Navy — Aviation — Juvenile literature.
[1. Fighter planes. 2. Airplanes, Military. 3. United States. Navy — Aviation.]
I. Title. II. Series: Baker, David, 1944- Military aircraft Library.
UG1242.F5B364 1989 88-13768
358.4′3 — dc19 CIP
AC

CONTENTS

Attack!

The British call them the Falkland Islands, and the Argentinians call them the Malvinas. This tiny group of islands in the South Atlantic, less than 300 miles off the coast of South America, was the scene of fighting between two armed countries in 1982. The Argentinians believed they had a claim to ownership of the islands, but the British had been there for several hundred years. When the Argentinians invaded the Malvinas in 1982, the British sent a task force of many ships to re-take the islands.

At about 9:40 on the morning of May 4, 1982, two Super Etendard strike planes of the Argentinian navy scrambled into the air following a report of British warships sighted close by the islands. Flying a spy mission 110 miles to the south, a Lockheed Neptune operated by Argentina had located the ships and radioed this information back to the Rio Grande air base on the mainland.

The British had two aircraft carriers to the southeast of the Malvinas, protected on the Argentinian side by twelve warships screening the valuable *flat-tops* from possible attack. Just 24 minutes after taking off, the two Etendards were refueled in mid-air by a KC-130 Hercules tanker plane that had taken off with the Etendards. The strike planes continued on their flight path, heading for the lead ships of the British fleet.

Built by Douglas, the Skyraider was developed at the end of World War Two and saw wide use in Vietnam.

A French navy Super Etendard seen here with an Exocet missile shortly before takeoff.

In contact with the Neptune, the Etendards dropped down to very low altitude in an attempt to escape detection. They momentarily popped up to 500 feet, switched on their *target radars*, saw nothing, and dropped down again. With added information from the Neptune, which could see the British fleet all the time, the Etendards adjusted their course. The next time they popped up they saw several targets on their radar screen. Each pilot selected one, fired an Exocet missile, and immediately turned away to escape. It was 11:04 in the morning.

On board the British ship, it was too late to do anything. The Exocet is a very effective weapon and flies to its target powered by a rocket motor. Within two minutes the missiles streaked to their targets. Fortunately for the British, the one that hit HMS *Sheffield* failed to explode, but the fire started by the rocket motor still burning caused the total loss of the ship. It sank a few hours later. The other missile headed straight for HMS *Yarmouth*, but its radar was disrupted by jamming signals from the warship.

This action is typical of the speed and efficiency of modern strike missions. It represents one type of sortie — naval strike planes against slow or stationary targets at sea with radar-guided, high-speed air-launched missiles. As it was, the

The Sea Harrier gave a good account of itself in the South Atlantic War.

Of these three planes, the two farthest from the camera are navy Sea Harrier strike planes.

The United States is developing the Harrier as the AV-8B strike aircraft.

attack on the British fleet could have had more significant results. If the Argentinian pilots had waited a few more minutes, they could have sent their missiles against the two aircraft carriers, much more valuable targets for the Argentinians.

Naval strike planes have other jobs and other missions, and land-attack missions are by far the most common. In land-attack missions naval fighters and strike planes attack land targets in support of ground operations involving armies of troops. It is the naval equivalent of *close air support* and ground attack, which are missions flown by the U.S. Air Force when supporting U.S. Army or U.S. Marine operations.

Land-attack missions were carried out on the occupied Malvinas by British Sea Harrier strike planes. They helped deliver strong attacks to relieve the British marines of much hard fighting. In one spectacular strike on the evening of May 28, 1982, three Sea Harriers of No. 1 Squadron, RAF, delivered a major punch on Goose Green, where 1,000 Argentinian soldiers were holding a fort and

Ships at sea are vulnerable to medium-range attack from missiles; the USS* Stark *was hit by a missile in the Persian Gulf.

***Naval task force commanders plan a strike on Libya from the carrier* Saratoga.**

an airfield. The next morning, the entire garrison surrendered.

The U.S. Marine Corp has bought the Sea Harrier in its license-built version, called the AV-8, made by McDonnell Douglas. The South Atlantic conflict of 1982 represents the range of naval strike options: ship attack and land attack. It also includes the two types of aircraft that today form the core of naval and marine strike capabilities: conventional takeoff and landing planes (where a runway is necessary to get the plane in the air or back to the ground) and vertical takeoff planes (like the AV-8).

Unlike the army, which calls on the air force to give air support to missions, the U.S. Navy and the marine corps have their own wings that go wherever they are needed. In this way, naval and marine aviation is more closely tied in with the military responsibilities of the respective services than with the conventional land and air forces. The navy has more operational strike planes than the marine corps.

Sea Legs

Built as a nuclear strike plane, the Rockwell Vigilante was one of the biggest planes ever to operate from the deck of an aircraft carrier.

What characterizes a navy strike plane? Toughness and muscle. While the U.S. operates a wide range of planes on land and flies anti-submarine patrols from continental bases, navy strike planes are flown exclusively from aircraft carriers. They must go where the battle fleet decides they are needed or where planners dictate they must be stationed. They work their daily chores in one of the toughest and roughest environments of any airplane anywhere.

Navy planes are catapulted into the air with enormous force and reach flying speed in two seconds flat. To get back down they suffer tremendous strain in what is called a controlled crash landing. Weather and flying conditions are sometimes appalling. Salt water, sea spray, and oil are never far away. The U.S. Navy never buys air force fighters and attack planes, because these planes are not strong enough to take the hard use and stress of navy carrier life. Navy planes are

The mainstay of naval strike operations for many years was the McDonnell Douglas F-4 Phantom.

Long-range carrier protection is provided today by the F-14 Tomcat built by Grumman Aerospace.

The Vought A-7 attack plane can carry both conventional and nuclear weapons.

All navy planes are built for quick access and speedy servicing.

The F/A-18 is built by McDonnell Douglas for combined fighter and attack duties.

sometimes bought for the air force, however. The McDonnell Douglas F-4 Phantom is the classic example.

The life of a navy strike plane is like that of no other airplane. Stressed far greater than land fighters, they carry enormous warloads and usually fight the toughest battles. They frequently operate alone and do not have the umbrella of protective cover from other planes that land fighters get. Navy strike planes are usually developed from large naval fighter planes, although there have been some spectacular departures from that trend.

One of the most extraordinary departures was the Rockwell Vigilante. Vigilante was the last of the atom-bomb planes built to carry out a heavy punch against cities and towns far inland. Until the mid-1960s, the navy wanted long-range nuclear bombers to serve as a *strategic nuclear deterrent*. Today that job is carried out for the navy by submarines carrying Poseidon or Trident ballistic missiles.

Vigilante was big. With a wing span of 53 feet and a length of 76 feet, it could eject a single, very large nuclear bomb from a rear-facing section of the fuselage. It had a range of 3,200 miles and a top speed of 1,385 MPH. With a maximum weight of 80,000 pounds, Vigilante was easily the heaviest warplane routinely deployed on aircraft carriers. It was assigned a role outside the normal responsibilities of the navy and marked the turning point to a more flexible role, where strike planes would be capable of a wider range of jobs.

The F/A-18 Hornet is capable of carrying out long-range strike missions form carriers anywhere in the world.

The one plane that came along in the 1960s to reflect that change was the F-4 Phantom. Tough and rugged, the Phantom was able to carry about eight tons of bombs and rockets for attack missions on land targets. It was used extensively by the navy as well as the marine corps and distinguished itself with the air force as noted earlier. In Vietnam, all three services used the Phantom with great effect. It frequently took a lot of battle damage from guns and *anti-aircraft rockets* and came home safely with its crew.

Today, all the navy Phantoms have been retired. Their place has been taken by other planes that have split the fighter and strike roles the F-4 carried out. The marine corps continues to operate the Phantom and has about 80 on hand, 60 of which carry out the fighter role. The other 20 are used as reconnaissance planes. The F-14 Tomcat serves the navy today as a long-range *interceptor*, and the strike work is done by A-7 Corsair attack bombers or F/A-18 Hornets. The Hornet also doubles as a short-range fighter for carrier defense.

Navy Strike

The most effective strike planes are not always the fastest, nor can they always carry the biggest load. The most flexible and accurate strike plane in the navy today is the Grumman A-6 Intruder. Grumman has had a long and proud history of building planes that are tough, reliable, and true performers. The A-6 is in that tradition and has been with the navy since 1963. It is likely to be in front-line service until well into the next century.

The navy wanted a low-level attack bomber capable of carrying conventional bombs, rockets and missiles, or nuclear weapons. This bomber had to be capable of carrying out its strike in any kind of weather, day or night. The specification leading to the A-6 was prepared in the mid-1950s, and Grumman got the contract to build the Intruder in 1957. Well over 600 Intruders have been built, and the plane has been purchased by the marine corps also.

Intruder saw extensive service in Vietnam, where it made a name for itself as a close air support plane. Planes that carry out close air support roles assist the army or the marine corps with military action on the ground. A *forward air controller* with a radio set hides in concealed undergrowth within sight of the target. From there he can talk to the pilots of the A-6s. The target may be a bridge where enemy units are crossing, or it may be a bunker or an artillery site where enemy field guns are pounding the ground units.

The air support mission is authorized at a high

Grumman Aerospace has built many navy planes, none more successful than the A-6 Intruder.

Navy strike pilots need good visibility when flying very fast.

Intruder provides good all-around visibility from its two forward crew seats.

This version of the Intruder has been modified for in-flight refueling through a curved probe on the nose.

Like all navy planes, Intruder must be catapulted into the air from a short flight deck.

level at the request of a local commander who finds he needs an air strike to knock out strong or heavily defended targets. The A-6s come in and carry out their strike with guidance from the forward air controller. This man can see the effect of the weapons dropped on the target and can advise other planes following whether the lead intruder is sufficiently accurate for the rest to use his bomb bursts as markers.

Close air support demands a tough plane that can look after itself, because it will most frequently be used in rough conditions. The usual approach made by these planes is to fly at very low altitude, hiding in the folds of hills and valleys. Positioned below could be several anti-aircraft *radar-guided guns* or missile sites, which the attacking force would want to avoid at all costs. Just before reaching the target area, the A-6 would climb rapidly, drop its weapons, and peel off to escape, once again at low altitude. The pilot would probably fly a winding course to avoid being hit by gunfire.

Because the support mission is being carried out on a moving battlefield, there would be little or no intelligence about the location of anti-aircraft units. They would probably consist of mobile gun and rocket positions that could change quickly as the battle's front line moved about. This major

An Intruder pilot does a circuit of his carrier before setting off on a simulated combat mission.

This version of the Intruder, known as the EA-6, is designed to jam enemy radar signals.

hazard facing A-6 pilots is typical of the threats navy pilots face on missions like this.

With such missions as a routine expectation, the A-6 came out as a compact attack plane with folding wings. These wings make storage easier in limited space aboard the aircraft carrier. The fuselage of the A-6 is 54 feet, 9 inches long. Extended, the wings span exactly 53 feet. Folded, they take up only 25 feet, 4 inches. The plane stands 16 feet, 2 inches high.

When empty, the A-6 weighs just over 13 tons, and with a maximum load it weighs 29.3 tons. The maximum carrier landing weight is 18 tons. This means that if the A-6 has to return before using up fuel or releasing its heavy load, the plane must jettison sufficient weight to get below the maximum landing weight. Maximum weapons load on pylons attached to the wings is a remarkable 9 tons.

The Intruder can carry a wide range of weapons. A typical load might be 28 500-pound bombs and two 300-gallon drop tanks with extra fuel. The drop tanks are jettisoned when the fuel they contain has been used up. Each pylon has the capacity to carry a weight of 3,600 pounds, and the A-6 can carry Sidewinder *air-to-air-missiles (AAM)* for self-defense against fighter planes if necessary. It carries no gun.

For certain missions, the Intruder will carry the Harpoon missile. This missile is guided to its target and flies on the propulsion of a rocket motor. Harpoon has a range of up to 75 miles and weighs just over 1,100 pounds. The A-6 can also carry HARM, a smaller missile with a range of 10 miles, weighing 807 pounds. These missiles are suited to particular mission requirements and are selected according to the job that needs to be done.

The navy has developed a guided missile called Skipper II, which the Intruder has been cleared to carry. This weapon is capable of sending a 1,000-pound warhead a distance of more than 10 miles at 700 MPH. It is very accurate and would be used against pinpoint targets, such as the span of a major viaduct or bridge. Because it is a *powered bomb*, the Intruder can drop it a long way from the target and avoid heavy concentrations of anti-aircraft defenses.

At the end of a mission, the Intruder must be able to land back on a heaving carrier deck in all kinds of weather.

The performance of the A-6 is based upon the design of the airframe and its two Pratt and Whitney *turbojet engines*, which together deliver a total maximum thrust of 18,600 pounds. The plane can extend its range by filling its fuel tanks from a tanker plane using a special *in-flight refueling probe* on the nose. How far the A-6 can fly on internal fuel depends on the weight of the bombs and missiles it carries. With a maximum warload the plane can fly just over 1,000 miles. Ferry range with jettisonable external fuel tanks is 3,245 miles.

The A-6 has a normal cruising speed of 474 MPH but can increase this to 644 MPH for a high-speed dash at very low level. Its good rate of climb, more than 7,000 feet a minute, comes in very handy when the plane has to get away in a

Like all navy planes, the Intruder has folding wings to limit the space it takes up on the carrier.

hurry. The aircraft has a ceiling of 42,000 feet and can land on only 1,710 feet of rough landing strip, or a very much shorter distance when pulled up sharply by the arrester wire spread across the deck of the carrier.

The Intruder really has no competitor, and the navy has organized a major development program to keep the plane in use for many years to come. Through the Intruder II program, an additional 150 planes will be purchased between now and 1995. The Intruder II will have bigger and more powerful engines, many modifications to its electronics and weapons control systems, and improved instruments for the two crew members. Intruder II will carry more fuel and have a much stronger wing. The new wing will be tougher and last longer than existing A-6 wings.

Some versions of the basic A-6 have been developed for other duties. One, a stretched Intruder, has been named the EA-6 Prowler. It operates as an *electronic spy plane* to seek out and jam enemy radars that might interfere with the attack planes on their demanding missions. Another version of the basic A-6 is the KA-6 *refueling tanker*, which refills navy planes in the air to give them extra range. A typical modern aircraft carrier would have 10 Intruders, 4 Prowlers and 4 tanker planes.

The other navy strike plane that has recently entered service is the McDonnell Douglas F/A -18 Hornet. It replaces the older A-7 Corsair and A-4 Skyhawk strike planes. The A-4 is discussed in the following section on marine corps attack planes. The Corsair first flew in 1965 and can lift more than 7 tons of weapons to its target, which may be up to 800 miles from the aircraft carrier. The navy still has more than 200 Corsairs in service.

A close-up of an AGM-84A HARM missile mounted to an aircraft on a carrier deck.

A Harpoon missile is fitted to the fuseage of an A-4 Skyhawk.

Skipper II low-level laser-guided bombs dropped from an A-6.

An F/A-18 with an AGM-84A Harpoon air-to-surface anti-ship missile under each wing.

The Hornet has been developed from the failed competitor for the air force lightweight fighter of the early 1970s. The winner was General Dynamics with the F-16 Fighting Falcon, but McDonnell Douglas took the YF-17 and substantially modified it into the F/A-18 Hornet. It entered service during 1983, and by the end of the decade around 700 will have been delivered to the U.S. Navy, the marine corps, and foreign customers. The navy alone will buy more than 1,000 Hornets.

The Hornet flew for the first time in November

All navy strike planes must have specially strengthened undercarriages to protect them from the shock of rough landing.

1978, and the production line was set up quickly after that. The first unit, formed at Naval Air Station Lemoore in California during November 1980, got its planes soon after, and began an intensive series of flight tests. Two Hornet squadrons formed for operational duty aboard the USS *Constellation* in February 1985 and the F/A-18 went to sea for the first time. Its designation describes its two roles. The F stands for fighter and the A stands for attack.

Like most navy planes, the Hornet has two engines to increase reliability. The open sea is no place to run out of engines. A single engine failure far from the safety of a carrier could be both embarrassing and dangerous. Two General Electric *turbofan engines*, each developing 8 tons of thrust, power the Hornet to a maximum speed of more than 1,100 MPH at high altitudes or about 750 MPH at low ones. With an internal fuel load of 1,700 gallons, the plane has a combat radius of about 660 miles for an attack mission. When used as a fighter the combat radius is cut to 460 miles.

The home of the strike plane, the only place to put a plane down far from land.

An EA-6B lands back on the carrier deck after a mission.

The combat radius is the distance from the carrier the plane can fly to carry out its job and return safely with a margin of fuel remaining in the tanks. When flying a ferry mission, where the most fuel-efficient speed and engine settings are used, the Hornet can fly 2,300 miles non-stop. It has a combat ceiling of 50,000 feet and a good rate of climb. The Hornet can lift a full weapons load of 8.5 tons on seven underwing and under-fuselage pylons.

The Hornet is 56 feet in length with a wing span of 37 feet, 6 inches (40 feet, 4 inches including wingtip missiles usually carried as standard defense against other fighters). Empty, the plane weighs 11.5 tons, and when fully loaded for an attack mission, it weighs 29.5 tons. This is very close to the maximum loaded weight of the A-6 Intruder, but the Hornet has a greater capacity for carrying weapons. While the Hornet is faster to its target, it does not have the range of the A-6.

Marine Air

The U.S. Marine Corp operates about 290 strike planes. Of these about 50 are Grumman A-6 Intruders, 100 are F/A-18 Hornets, 80 are McDonnell Douglas A-4 Skyhawks, and the rest are McDonnell Douglas AV-8B Harrier IIs, the revolutionary vertical takeoff planes. The marines also have about 70 AH-1 Sea Cobra *attack helicopters.* In all, the marines possess more than 450 combat planes and 80 armed helicopters. The rest of the range includes trainers, tankers, tanker planes, and troop transporting helicopters.

The McDonnell Douglas A-4 Skyhawk is one of the world's most successful airplanes. It was in continuous production for 26 years, between 1954, when the prototype first flew, and 1980. The Skyhawk has been the standard light attack plane for the navy for 20 years, and it has served the marine corps well in peace and war. From the outset, the plane was designed to be lightweight and high-performance. Its designer, Ed Heinemann, was concerned about the increasing weight of fighter and attack planes and focused on a simple design that would not be heavy.

The navy and the marine corps wanted a plane that could carry a 1-ton warload, including nuclear weapons, fly 345 miles to drop its bombs and return, and achieve a top speed of 500 MPH. It took Heinemann two weeks to draw up the design and achieve better performance than was specified! The final version of the Skyhawk can carry 4.5 tons of weapons, fly a combat radius of 920 miles, and reach a top speed of 670 MPH. The customer had specified a maximum load weight of 15 tons. The Skyhawk bettered that with a maximum weight of 13.5 tons.

Designed in the 1950s, the A-4 Skyhawk was one of the most outstanding fighter designs of all time, achieving light weight and high performance for its size.

The Skyhawk has operated in many areas of the world and in several different conflicts.

The A-4 has a length of 40 feet, 3 inches , which includes a single Pratt and Whitney turbojet engine delivering a thrust of 4.2 tons. It has a wing span of only 27 feet, 6 inches. Five pylon locations provide ample space to hang weapons, and the plane comes with two standard 20mm cannons and 400 rounds of ammunition. There are no sophisticated guidance and weapons control systems, and it represents the typical attack concept of the 1950s. Fly over the target, line it up with the aiming sights, and drop the weapons.

Because of its comparatively low cost, the Skyhawk is popular among foreign customers. Several countries fly this plane. By the time production ceased, McDonnell Douglas had built no fewer than 2,960 for U.S. and overseas clients. Several versions have been produced with additional systems included for particular requirements. There was even a trainer version with two seats.

McDonnell Douglas is an aerospace corporation of two merged companies. McDonnell Aircraft built several planes for the U.S. Navy and the U.S. Marine Corp, the most famous of which was the F-4 Phantom. Douglas Aircraft, too, had a fine record of achievement with navy planes, designing many jet fighter and attack planes like the Skyhawk. It is fitting, therefore, that the most revolutionary attack plane in service today should be developed by this corporation.

This unique attack plane began life in the 1950s at a British aircraft manufacturer called Hawker Siddeley (now part of British Aerospace). Hawker Siddeley designed a plane that could take off and land vertically. If developed, they believed the concept would revolutionize air power. No longer would planes be limited to operating from long concrete runways. Combat planes could operate from fields, forest clearings, and any place where there was space to go straight up and down like a helicopter. Like a helicopter, too, the plane could hover and be made to go backwards and sideways.

First developed as the experimental P.1127, the plane demonstrated that the principle was correct. A plane could be made to do those extraordinary things. It was then adapted into the Kestrel, which had more features of a combat plane. The Kestrel's designers thought it should be developed further into a bigger plane with higher performance. That idea was dropped, and the Kestrel was finally sold to the British Royal Air Force as the Harrier. It was soon nicknamed the "Jump Jet," for obvious reasons.

Interest from the United States began in the late 1960s, when the marine corps ordered 20 planes under the designation of AV-8A. The initial letter A stood for attack and the V for vertical take-off. The first order was extended, and the marines eventually got 100 AV-8As, with most being built under license by McDonnell Douglas in the United

The A-4 has operated as a fighter and several versions have flown as attack planes and trainers.

Skyhawk can carry a variety of bombs and rockets including conventional or nuclear weapons.

States. The AV-8A suited the marines well, because they needed a plane to support troop operations in remote places, capable of amphibious landings on coastal strips.

McDonnell Douglas was eager to develop the plane further. They gave it a new wing design and an improved engine built by Pratt and Whitney under license from Rolls Royce in England. The AV-8 was virtually redesigned to include improvements that became obvious during the several years of operating the plane. It was modified to meet the requirements of the marines, and the new version was called the AV-8B Harrier II.

Altogether, the marines will buy around 320

Douglas engineer E.H. Heinemann was the A-4's brilliant designer.

An A-4F Skyhawk fires a Shrike missile.

AV-8Bs, of which 28 will be two-seat trainers. The AV-8B is significantly different from the AV-8A, which followed the original British Harrier design. Yet the AV-8B still retains all the principal features of that first historic plane, the P.1127, that was designed more than 30 years ago. While not a successful project for the British, who stopped putting money into further development, it has certainly been a success for McDonnell Douglas, who took it to a new level of performance.

The basic plane is small, with a length of 46 feet, 4 inches and a wing span of 30 feet, 4 inches. It stands 11 feet, 7 inches high and is supported on the ground by a strange set of wheels. Instead of the normal nose wheel and two main wheels, the Harrier II has two main wheels in the center of the fuselage, one near the front and one near the back. To prevent the plane from tipping over sideways, it has an outrigger leg and wheel midway along each wing. In this way the plane stands on four separate wheels.

The most revolutionary feature of the Harrier II is its incredible engine, designed with rotating nozzles to deflect its powerful thrust down or back.

Because the plane is supported during takeoff entirely by the thrust of its engine, it must be very powerful and reliable. If the engine were to fail during the time the plane is ascending or descending, the AV-8 would crash to the ground.

To overcome gravity, the engine must have more thrust than the weight of the plane. Empty, the AV-8B weighs 6.5 tons, but with a full load of fuel and weapons on board it weighs a maximum of 9.5 tons. The engine, called the F402, is modeled after the Rolls Royce Pegasus engine that was developed originally for the first experimental plane of this type. With a thrust of 11 tons, it is easily capable of lifting the AV-8B off the ground.

The AV-8B is built to fly straight up and down when taking off or landing, but it can also take off from a runway like a conventional plane. The fuselage and wings are able to support more weight than their 9.5-ton limit for vertical takeoff; extra weapons or fuel can be loaded to a maximum

The marines operate A-4 Skyhawks as well as the navy.

The Skyhawk has an incredible performance, which is even better than the navy's original specification.

The range of the A-4 can be extended by special drop tanks carrying extra fuel.

The A-4 has been developed into several versions; the Skyhawk II seen here is flying over rugged terrain.

weight of 15 tons if the plane is taking off from a runway. A combination of slightly extra weight and short takeoff roll is preferred, unless the situation absolutely demands that the plane must take off vertically.

Because the Harrier II has such startling capabilities, its sheer performance in terms of speed and range is not very great. It does not have to be. Attack planes in a close support role should live and work with the army or marine corps units they are attached to. The AV-8B can do this better than any other plane, because it can usually accompany the ground forces wherever they go. It needs carrying capacity, hitting power, and reliability, and has all three in great quantity.

Weapons include a five-barrel General Electric 25mm *gatling gun* under the fuselage and a variety of bombs and rockets. Six pylon positions under the wings and one under the fuselage provide ample space for hanging various weapons, up to 3.3 tons for vertical takeoff or 8.5 tons for short, rolling takeoff. Up to 16 500-pound general purpose bombs can be carried, as well as combinations of rockets, missiles, fuel tanks, and *electronic jamming pods*. The jamming pods are used to confuse enemy radar.

Maximum speed for the AV-8B is 650 MPH in level flight close to the ground, and the operational radius of action permits the AV-8B to take off, fly 550 miles, drop its load, and return. For air combat missions where it is looking for enemy strike planes to attack, the plane can fly 115 miles from base, spend three hours in the air on patrol, and return. With four jettisonable fuel tanks, the plane can ferry itself a distance of 2,440 miles.

In 1987, McDonnell Douglas and British Aerospace agreed to develop the Harrier III, or Super Harrier. Its engine, delivering 12.5 tons of thrust, will be more powerful than the Harrier II's. In addition, it will have improved radar and the

To give the navy flexibility, the vertical takeoff AV-8B is a development of the British Harrier used in the South Atlantic war of 1982.

Possibly the most famous of all navy strike planes, the F-4 Phantom has seen extensive service with many air forces throughout the world.

Although primarily designed as a fighter, the Phantom is equally capable of delivering rockets, bombs, or missiles on ground targets.

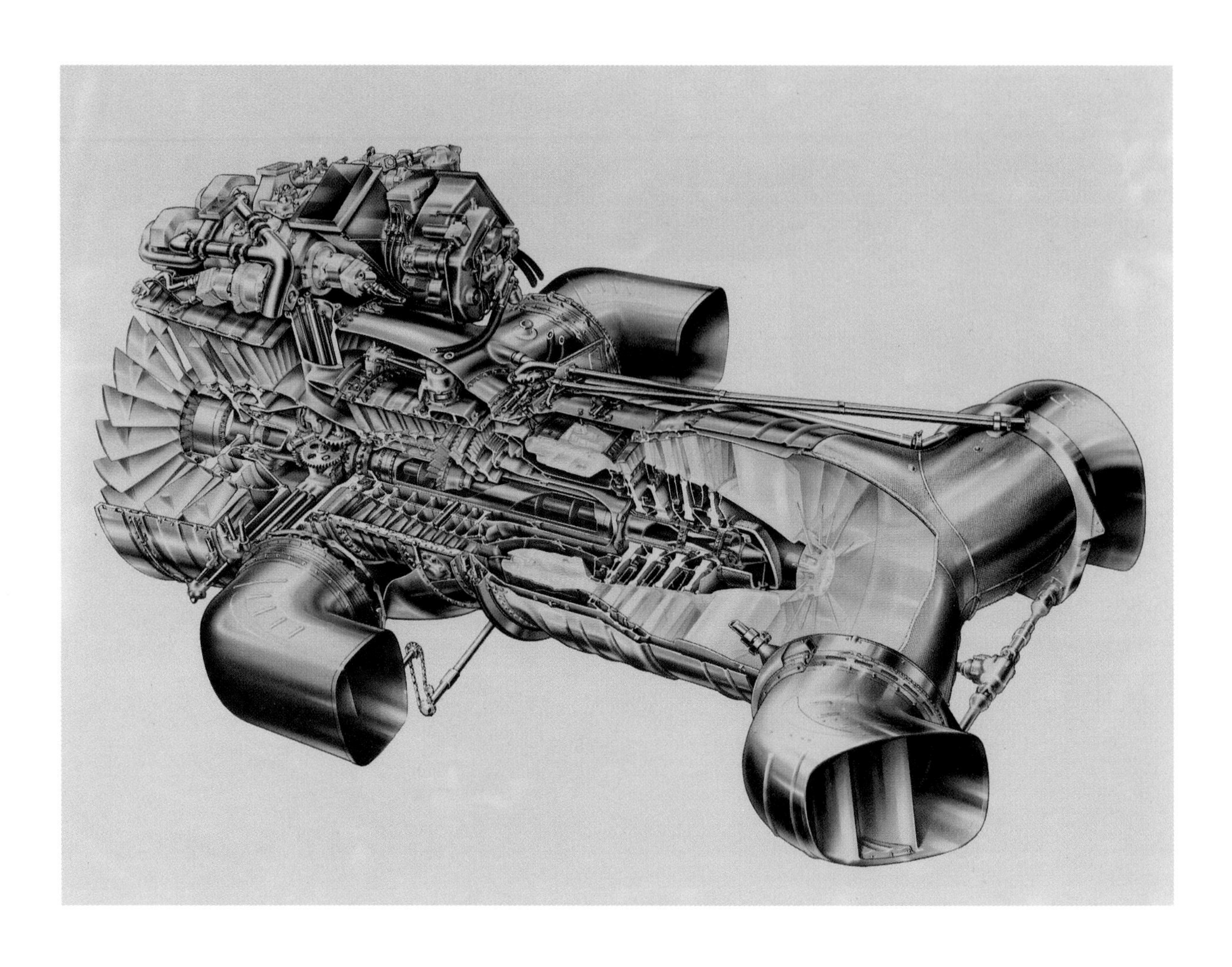

The secret of the AV-8B is the Pegasus engine, capable of giving the plane vertical thrust.

ability to launch missiles to targets over the horizon. Until that time however, the AV-8B remains the only plane of its kind in the world, and one that brings new flexibility to close air support for marine operations.

The navy operates carrier-based strike planes, and the marine corps operates conventional and vertical takeoff planes deployed to stay with the ground units and support them. The marines also have about 70 attack helicopters, all Bell AH-1 Sea Cobras. The Sea Cobra is a two-seat light attack helicopter for use in a conflict to support ground troops and knock out enemy gun posts or radar units.

The Sea Cobra is just over 48 feet long, and the rotor has a diameter of 48 feet. It weighs 4 tons loaded and has a top speed of 200 MPH, making it suitable for fast hit-and-run missions. The AH-1 belongs to a long family of Bell gunships, of which the army has more than 1,000. They were developed as a direct result of experience in Vietnam and have a reputation for tough, rugged reliability.

The Sea Cobra has a normal operating height of

around 10,000 feet and can fly about 380 miles on internal fuel. The helicopter can carry rocket launchers and missiles in addition to its standard armament. Standard armament consists of a standard General Electric gun in a special turret just under the nose. The 20mm gun, called the M197, has three barrels. It is a lightweight version of the Vulcan cannon fitted to several modern fighters, such as the navy F-14 Tomcat and the air force F-15 Eagle and F-16 Fighting Falcon. The air force also uses the gun in the tail of the giant B-52 bomber.

The marine corps operates three versions of the Sea Cobra, each an improvement over the previous one. The most recent version provides considerable increase in performance. The original Sea Cobra had a Pratt and Whitney engine delivering 1,800 horsepower. The latest version has two General Electric engines with a combined output of 3,200 horsepower. Changes to the electronics

A U.S. Marine Corp ground technician checks an AGM-65E Maverick missile prior to AV-8B flight tests.

The AV-8B carries a specially modified wing that gives the plane greater lift than the basic British Harrier.

and the radar permits new types of missions to be flown.

The marine corps operates its Sea Cobras for a range of tasks, including anti-armor flights where it hunts for tanks and *armored personnel carriers*. It is also used for escorting troop-carrying helicopters and for carrying out reconnaissance of enemy-held territory. The Sea Cobra can go on search missions where it is looking for targets that may need the attention of the A-4 or the AV-8B. In this way it helps extend the eyes of the marine corps for planning ground operations "over the hill."

The navy and the marine corps operate self-contained strike planes for missions against enemy targets at sea and on land. These strike planes are unique because they are capable of performing a task without calling upon the army or the air force for support. The U.S. Navy and the U.S. Marine Corp have some of the finest airplanes in the world, and the marines' Harrier II is the most revolutionary. Navy and marine strike planes are not designed for the big nuclear wars but for the common forms of conflict where quick action can prevent escalation into a major war. By participating at that level, they provide a valuable and necessary service.

Operated by the marines, the AV-8B can get close to the battle front by operating out of small clearings.

The marine corps operate the AH-1 Sea Cobra at sea for land attack support operations.

Crew members prepare to attach a Sidewinder missile to a marine corps AH-1 Sea Cobra helicopter.

An A-6 Intruder is fitted with Tacit Rainbow, a device designed to locate, attack, and destroy enemy radar installations at sea or on shore.

GLOSSARY

Air-to-air missiles (AAM)	Missiles launched from aircraft to attack enemy aircraft in the air.
Anti-aircraft rockets	Rockets launched from the ground or from aircraft designed to destroy other aircraft in the air.
Armored personnel carriers	Tracked or wheeled vehicles protected with armor plate and used to carry soldiers or infantry men.
Attack helicopters	Helicopters designed and operated to attack other helicopters or light aircraft.
Close air support	The use of aircraft to attack ground targets in support of surface operations.
Electronic jamming pods	Pods of electronic equipment carried under the wing or fuselage of electronic warfare planes to jam and confuse enemy radar.
Electronic spy plane	An aircraft equipped to detect and jam enemy radar sets before they can pick up incoming aircraft.
Flat-top	The popular name given to an aircraft carrier.
Forward air controller	A foot soldier, hidden in a position close to enemy targets, who reports by radio to friendly forces the results of attacks made by strike planes.
Gatling gun	A type of gun in which several barrels are positioned together in a cluster. As a barrel fires, the cluster rotates into position for the next barrel. This action continues while the gun is being used.
In-flight refueling probe	A fixed probe, usually attached to the nose of an aircraft, that can be connected with a flexible hose from a tanker plane to transfer fuel in flight.
Interceptor	A fighter plane designed to attack approaching enemy aircraft.
Powered bomb	A bomb attached to a propulsive device that boosts it to its target.
Radar-guided guns	Anti-aircraft guns linked to radar scanners that control the direction and angle of fire.
Refueling tanker	An aircraft that carries special equipment for refueling other aircraft in flight.
Strategic nuclear deterrent	A nuclear weapon with awesome power to destroy, designed and held to discourage others from waging war.

Target radars	Radars that are designed to track targets when general surveillance radars have indicated their presence. Target radars help identify a specific target for attack by specific weapons.
Turbofan engine	A jet engine with blades arranged in a circle like a fan to increase the amount of air delivered to the combustion chamber.
Turbojet engine	A pure jet engine that burns a mixture of fuel and air, with compressor blades to control the flow of this mixture through the engine inlet.

INDEX

Page references in *italics* indicate photographs or illustrations.